More Praise for Mexican Dinosaur

"This is a Texas sized snake fist punching old folktales & inventing new ones. These poems are for the weirdos, the outsiders, the nerds who think they're cool & the cool kids who think they're nerds. It's a road map for people who find themselves in rock & hip hop lyrics & stand in the intersection of being Mexican, being Mexican-American, being from Texas & being from San Antonio, which are all similar & yet very different. Martinez will teach you old magic chants & choruses of A Tribe Called Quest, all the while driving down Highway 151 with his fist in the air like the last scene in your favorite movie."
- Bonafide Rojas, Poet, Musician & Author of Notes On The Return To The Island

"Modern but grounded in the history of South Texas, this book feels at home in the duality of Mexican-American life. It reads like you're getting good chisme on a front porch."
- Natasha Hernandez, Editor of St. Sucia Zine

"Rooster said what many of us from the Barrio think and he was vulnerable about experiences that we may be afraid to talk about. It's charming, moving, unapologetic and all of that stuff that makes us Mexican Americans dope. The line in the poem "Loconuts" *My neighbor sells drugs and he's polite as shit,* should make you want to buy this book. Five snaps out of five snaps."
- Jose Arredondo, Spectrum News Texas Journalist

Mexican Dinosaur

POEMS BY
C.L. "ROOSTER" MARTINEZ

WRITE ABOUT NOW PUBLISHING

Mexican Dinosaur

© 2023 C.L. "Rooster" Martinez

All rights reserved. No part of this publication may be reproduced, stored in a retrieval system or transmitted in any form or by any means, electronic, mechanical, photocopying, recording or otherwise without the prior permission of the author.

Editor: Ayokunle Falomo

Editor-in-Chief & Typesetting: M.R. "Chibbi" Orduña

Associate Editor: Amir Safi

Cover Design: Morgan Williams

Published by:

Write About Now Publishing, Texas, USA

www.wanpoetry.com | @wanpoetry

Print ISBN: 978-0-9906127-4-2

Ebook ISBN: 978-0-9906127-5-9

Printed in USA

Set in Amatica SC and ITC Berkeley Oldstyle STD

If you are viewing this publication as an ebook, so that you may experience this book as it was intended, the publishers recommend you scale your font so that the text below appears on one complete line.

This line is the size guide & should fit completely on one line only.

For the misfits

"How will we ever recover from colonization, but to reclaim what we can, where we can, how we can, with hopes that our culture might better reauthenticate in the next generation?"

-Stephanie Elizondo Griest, "Dia De Muertos", Nepantla Families.

Rasquache: (ra-skwa-ch-eh) making art or giving a new function to something that would conventionally be considered broken or otherwise useless.

Rasquachismo: a theory developed by Chicano scholar Tomás Ybarra-Frausto to describe "an underdog perspective, a view from los de abajo" which uses "hybridization, juxtaposition, and integration" as a means of empowerment and resistance. -Wikipedia

Contents

Tabasco	13
If You Want to Know what it's like to Be Mexican	14
MX)(AM	15
Slaughterhouse Mouth	19
Black Fur	21
Recetas (Salsa Verde)	22
The only thing I would order from Taco Bell is a Baja Blast Mountain Dew and that's only because I like the color	23
Top Gun: Maverick plays on mute as 99 luftballons go by	25
Scope (an erasure about Los Rinches)	27
I'm tired of these schizophrenic gods	28
Pachanga! Pachanga! Pachanga! (Jan 2020)	29
If you want to know what it's like to be Mexican	33
Toque	34
How to Kill a Caveman	36
Mad Money	38
The Fourth Generation	41

IF YOU WANT TO KNOW WHAT IT'S LIKE TO BE MEXICAN	44
LOCONUTS	45
RECETAS (ARROZ ROJO)	49
I'M A SHITTY GARDENER	50
THE LAST TIME I SAW YOU	52
IF YOU WANT TO KNOW WHAT IT'S LIKE TO BE MEXICAN	54
BAD BIRD MÁGICO	55
GODS LIKE US	56
BO-DE-GAS	57
JURY DUTY BLUES	59
RAIN, HUMO, RAIN	61
KOOL KOOL GUY	62
MY BANK EMAILS ME AND ASKS IF I'M READY TO PLAN FOR MY RETIREMENT	65
BARRIO YARD SALE	67
THE LEGEND OF MARK	71
MEXICAN DINOSAUR	74
IF YOU WANT TO KNOW WHAT IT'S LIKE TO BE MEXICAN	75

Ten Things About South Texas of which I am Certain	76
Sunflower Road	80
I got kicked out of college three times and still arrived on this side of glass	81
Chingasos from Above	84
A Confederacy of Ghosts Still Here	85
If You Want to Know what it's like to be Mexican	88
I Grew Tired of the Old Gods, so I Made New Ones	89
Somos Cosmicanos	92
Wasim Akram and Allen Iverson on the Blacktop	93
Acknowledgements	98
About the Author	99
Suggested Playlist	100

Tabasco

A curse word lept from my six year old lips
To my father's ears
& begot Tabasco

Demanding my tongue
Father gave back a fire

Why anything

Should exist so hot in the mouth

I didn't understand

But I understood

I could survive pain
                                      then & after
& some words

   I n c i n e r a t e

If you want to know what it's like to be Mexican

I.

I don't know

        or

                at least

                              they all tell me

I

    will

        never

            know

MX][AM

In the earth-shattering bio pic: *Selena*
Edward James Olmos says:
being mexican-american
you must work twice as hard–
be more mexican than mexicans, more american than americans

I don't know who wrote that line of script
anymore than I know who wrote my barrio
but I know I am mexican-american   hyphenated af
and I'm tired of working twice as hard
to impress both mexicans & americans

I'm mexican-american
and I know I enjoy yoga star wars hip hop and spring rolls

I know I don't speak spanish well
a boll that pricks many mexicanos
tongues blotted back and broken for so many gods
I am thankful for sacred language
that survives any apocalypse
so be thankful
what I can speak strikes for you and not at you   cabron

every summer I see Spain and Tenochtitlan in tan lines
I know the blood that makes my complexion new and ruined

yet still this skin as light as it is is a safety net I respect
yet still to this day in this very state

mi piel mi pelo my last name
are made outcasts in places my family knew as home
forever

I know the gravity of borders
how they arise from air and fall to earth from mad skies
the death behind manifest destiny
lines drawn and defined by deranged gods

I know a conqueror's kiss means well in history books
because it is written in conqueror's ink
I know there are a million ways to die
and a billion ways to scratch people out

I know I get bent out of shape when chingos of people
ask where are you from?
I say San Antonio
they say: yeah but where are you really from?
I say: well I come from Wu-Tang Clan
and throwing hands if you don't stop with the stupid questions

I know you should not come at me like you're one of my *essays*
if your not one of my *eses*

I know there are those who hate what I stand for
without a clue as to what I stand for
I know what I stand for is the truth–
baseball and soccer are boring as hell

I know this country does not have an immigration
problem
it has a xenophobic attitude towards immigrants
problem

I don't know why the only recognizable heroes
who speak for me in most media are:
Cheech & Chong, Jennifer Lopez, Lin-Manuel Miranda, and Sophia Vergara
(all of which, besides Cheech, are not mexican)

I know I'm mexican-american
and we invented the bicycle and sex with the lights on

(and I made those last two facts up)

but I do want a smooth lowrider in my life
I don't care if you think ranflas are tacky

I know big trucks with lift kits and fake rubber nuts hanging from
the trailer hitch is tacky

I know a minivan with stick figure window stickers of your entire
family is tacky

dare me to be anything different and you'll be let down,
but come around my barrio and see me

bumping A Tribe Called Quest with fresh spring rolls
but you won't catch me working double to be rejected twice

Slaughterhouse Mouth

You visit a new city
going out of your way
to meet someone
who looks like   you.

A torn map
falls from your lips
anytime   you
try   speech.

Where you come from,   la gente
saw   este país
bleed your tongue
rot   ruined meat.

You are not familiar
with never being familiar.

The sound of your tongue raises   preguntas.
Is it so hard to imagine
that you never immi-

grated to this country,
but this country immigrated
hard across your family?
To many, you are a bad spell,

confused butterfly migration,
a stolen voice, a bloody mouth.

You stand in a new city
like a folk tale in an abattoir.

Black Fur

I had mustache beginnings before eleven years old.
Magnum PI caliber taco meat by fifteen.
Bird's nests in all crevices.
I learned early how a yellow Bic, single-blade razor cuts and uproots
the animal from the manscape.
Ingrown and pocked, I am a moon under curls and tangles.
Hygiene is the Colonizer's second word after God, before Savage.
Black jaguar under a moon is the cleanest killing god.
The mossy tree or the jaguar in the canopy—
I am uncertain which I am, but neither were meant for civilization's dress code.
Shears and razors carve out a groomed gentleman
from the beast with midnight fur and glowing eyes.
Does the world remain wild to the boys with a foot still in the jungle?

Recetas
(Salsa Verde)

        lay it

        on anything you consume
        like home

        on everything you scorch
        and keep

        serrano peppers submerge
        the mouth in its own green
        heritage you eat what the elders
        teach learning so much about
        pain (a source a genesis point)
        tears & screaming
        held back
        like all memories
        revisiting them
        only
        out
        of duty

THE ONLY THING I WOULD ORDER FROM TACO BELL IS A BAJA BLAST MOUNTAIN DEW AND THAT'S ONLY BECAUSE I LIKE THE COLOR

To a company
that once thought "run for the border"
was a great marketing slogan,
you have enough cheesy sins to atone for.

Like most conquerors, you hid behind a mission facade
with white promises. You built a hardshell dynasty
on cheap ground beef and shredded American cheese,
Spanish guitars and commercial voice actors
whooo taaaaalk liiiike deeeees.

Yo quiero reparations, puto—and not for myself
but for the Mitla Cafe.

Taco Bell was founded by Glen Bell in San Bernardino.
After a failed hotdog and burger stand,
Glen saw the always bustling Mitla Cafe across the street and said,
"Eureka," a bell
which rang like "Conquest."
The folks at Mitla taught Bell
the alchemy of turning affordable food into generational wealth.

The rest is, as they say, basura—
basura tacos, basura history, basura marketing schemes.

For a company that sold meat that couldn't qualify as "meat,"
I have a beef, free of charge, extra dollop of big mad guac.

This time, we stamp out colonizer tacos
like Moctezuma should have.
This time, we unerase the Mitla Cafe
and throw Flamin' Hot® Cool Ranch® Doritos® Locos Tacos Supreme®
for $2.49 into the watery hell of the Gulf of California.

Top Gun: Maverick plays on mute as 99 luftballons go by

in this bar and in this Lone Star beer
i come to genuinely understand America

& i understand the sweet and sour of American-Chinese food
& the mismatch oversalted seasoning of Taco Bell
& the great exodus from life to the Metaverse

& wanting the dream as portrayed
and not as the country in therapy
mavericks don't require self-examination
mavericks require you suit up and fight the good fight

& i understand the good fight is code
for whatever side we're on in all conflicts
America gentrified the word freedom
perfected its taste like chocolate and nacho cheese
with dick-shaped jets and phallic bombs flaming across heaven
arcing death at unnamed uncountried evils

& maverick is the call-sign for every white guy without borders
& so many men take it as permission to be louder engines
& every insubordination justified if you withstand the G-force
& luftballons doesn't translate to red balloons
but the red makes so much sense
when the war is fake

& in your head
& you always win

& the ashes grow taller wings
& the idea of America fits neatly in a small flag-draped box

Scope (an erasure about Los Rinches)

San Diego, Tex. Jan 26, 1919

Hon. Canales

Austin, Tex.

My dear sir—I note with satisfaction that you are bringing into notice the injustice done by that lawless band of highwaymen known as Rangers. Twice within the months they have "shot up" this town. They have no regard for either the civil or military laws. They make their own out of a bottle, it used to be old Rippy it is mescale now. Seriously I've seen them drunk and abusive without the least excuse for it. They have abused me and I have appealed to the ADJ for relief. I can tell you of many instances to my personal knowledge of their lawless practices. If you wish. I am sure that they are the German Propagandists—they keep strife between the U.S. & Mexico they harass the lives out of the Mexican speaking citizens. The Germans are alone of strangers to find welcome to this part of Tex. Many men went to Mexico not to avoid the service of the U.S. but to avoid the inevitable unwarranted assault and arrest by the Rangers. It was and still is a reign of terror. They are in to everything, even civil cases. I can give you detailed accounts of their frightfulness here if you wish

Respectfully

Mrs. Virginia Yeager

I am Chairman Women Suffragists of this Co.

I'M TIRED OF THESE SCHIZOPHRENIC GODS

How come I pray to Tlaloc and it rains,
but every time I pray to Jesus, the fucking cops show up?

How come my mother gives all our blessing to God
but takes all our pendejadas out on our head?

How come a nun whup my ass
when I questioned why a daughter of god
would make a little girl cry?

How come the holy spirit don't stop my need to masturbate?
Does god walk with me then too? Does that make all sex group sex?

Are the gods not forwarding our prayers to the right diety's inbox?

How come Columbus or Hitler or Trump
never caught a lightning bolt in the foot
but we had our feet cut off?

Pachanga! Pachanga! Pachanga! (Jan 2020)

y'all It was crazy,
I was at a New Year's Eve party and I don't know
if "Get up, Stand up" was playing or
John Lennon's "Imagine"

but the party was rocking!
rocking like the pacifists found the formula for peace
rocking like the vegans convinced the whole world to swear off meat

rocking like Tupac and Biggie came BACK from the afterlife
and told the masses that the secret to happiness is sagging your jeans

and it was open bar and no cover charge
and we had two turn-tables and 4 billion microphones

and the fear of a global pandemic was nowhere near our lungs

the party was rocking like Jesus started a poetry slam
(and not a lot of people showed up to support)
but it still went hard and you're a sucker if you missed it

and Global Warming cooled the fuck out because Ice-T
from Law & Order SVU looked up at the sky and said:
"Yo G. Warming, knock that shit off."
AND THE SHIT KNOCKED OFF!!

and the bullet makers began making flower seeds

and the bomb makers began making fireworks & pinatas
and all the kids in cages
were not real kids but muppet kids

in an elaborate social experiment
to show our lack of compassion
and we realized the err of our ways

and then 300 million of us!
busted through the Southern Border Wall like the Kool-Aid Man
bringing Ben and Jerry's ice cream to all the niños

—because they're global niños now—
and this party knows! no! borders!

the party was rocking like women could catch a fucking break
like Black women could catch like two fucking breaks

like LGBTQ now stood for Let's Go Back to Quiznos—
because we all abided by the rules of proper allyship,
and gay, straight, a-sexual, bi, demi, pan
or whomever know that Quiznos is fucking awesome

and every drunk Kyle from sea to shining sea could see untouched
drywall and not want to punch a hole in it

and nobody broke a lamp

and it was a party without war

and I held my true Love's hand
and it looked like everyone
(and I'm not saying that to sound deep but to say:
that night, we all stopped seeing faces worthy of our anger)

and no, there wasn't an orgy,
but the sex that did go down was hella consensual

and I didn't know what to call anybody at this party
a friend
a stranger
people
spinning through the cosmos together
and hoping not to have to clean up after

but I spilled some Doritos
and a Roomba came almost immediately
because sometimes I make messes in this universe too

and at midnight
a kid blew out candles that looked like maga hats on a birthday cake
and made a wish

that didn't matter because the future looked brighter than any wish

and maybe all this is a wish
for an entire generation of kids
to be born into a world where they never have to throw a fist
and we called them
Generation   Y--can't-this-be-real-now?

IF YOU WANT TO KNOW WHAT IT'S LIKE TO BE MEXICAN

II.

estás aquí   de este lado

quieres estar ahí
                de ese lado

                y   ni lado
                te quiere

por eso miramos hacia los cielos
como los cantos de los grillos

                        ***

you are here   *on this side*
you wish to be there
                on that side

                and   *neither side*
                loves you

therefore we look up to the heavens
like the songs of crickets

Toque

Chibbi hands me instructions to Monopoly Deal
and I am useless / The others who know this game
speak a lexicon I am unfamiliar with / the jargon of game night
Eventually, I say, stop telling, play, I'll learn as we go

Two hands in and Crazyface takes stock
of my understanding / admires how quickly
the language comes to make sense as it is
dolled out over golden brown, room temp chicken wings

Chips and mango salsa / my tactile education / I touch things and they make sense
I am speaking in game night / Given a book /
I am useless / put in an institution / I am Einstein or insane

I visit Laredo often / put palms on the ground
the radiation reaching out to me / it is the closest
I get to Mexico / a land / my family says they
can teach me / they hand me books / and I am useless

they hand me photos / and I am useless
I hold my grandmother's hands / and I am in Eagle Pass
an artist / a young woman / I hold a gun or gold
and I am American / I am an institution /

I hold San Antonio / and I am a blessing / I am food best served
at room temperature / a game night /
I put my hands on everything / a useful reflex /
to hold ghosts / and I am not a poet

I write into words / what my hands see
The world is a surface to be touched /
It radiates and when we learn / I hold my friends
and I do not need instructions to their grief

How to Kill a Caveman

I
save the Earth
like Superman, GI Joe or Jesus | always a man
in the stories | propaganda pulled out
patriarchy pulp pages | biblical man ink
fossilizing the fables and myths |
but what if | Adam bit | the apple and lied about it?

II
A soft boy is a man eroded by trauma until he is all exposed roots.
He wants the peace of a flower in the face of a life of war.
A hard boy is a man
who punches problems out of [existence, a wall, another boy]
makes war his life, sword sworn.

III
I am somehow both these men—
shield and blade raised on messages and myths.

IIII
In nature, there can only be one alpha.
Ergo, alpha male culture is actually a majority of betas
playing pretend—
Men fearful of finding poems in their heart.

IIII̶
this is a poem

𝍦 I
there are people lucky I write poems

𝍦 II
I write poems so as to not hit people, to survive the paradox of being
flameproof while swallowing cinders, to drive a muscle car so fast my
demons blur in the rearview.

𝍦 III
In 9th grade, a 12th grader told me freshmen were on the menu.
That as soon as lunch was over, an onslaught was coming. When he
walked away to his lunch table, I busted a tray over his head because
fuck bullies, fuck seniors, and fuck thinking he could punk me.
I wanted to cry instead of cheer but fear of showing anything but
turned my tears into the flimsiest crown of the weakest kingdom.

𝍦 IIII
An 18 year old boy tells me
he'd be ashamed to bring even his suicidal feelings to his friends.
I tell him, he needs new friends.

𝍦 𝍦
Men: most of us were never kings.
We were the disposable pawns of kings.
The victims of prima nocta and empires that stole our sons.
Men: get therapy,
kill your caveman,
win the fight with the real phantoms
we haunt our homes with.

MAD MONEY

I was 16 or 17, and I don't know how much I took.
This isn't a confession—maybe, it is.

I justified it because the owner was a piece of shit—
talked to brown folx sideways—
never to but always at

like he had that boiling water in his throat,
rampant round these parts, that'd
bubble over, scald.   He'd catch it before it'd spill out
or would glimmer behind his eyes.

I am not Robin Hood nor he the Sheriff—

but once upon a different yet same shit day,
the owner threw the teenager's school clothes in a grease lined trash can.
He asked who they belonged to—the clothes.

I tell him, my friend—who just left school to be here to work for him.
The owner slighted that space was taken,
even for a second, in a near empty dining room,

twisted into a green confederacy
—something we know around here.
He's sending a message.
I know, Mrs. Jones works fingers into overnight shifts
at the grocery to keep her son clean.

I know the owner has children who eat
for free when the mood strikes.

He slams the door to the kitchen–message received.
I dig out my friend's pressed jeans and white button up from the
discarded brown french fries and burger grease.

When my friend returns, I tell him.
He stands stuck in the minimum wage uniform they give you
upon hiring,
the one you return when they fire you or you've had enough.

He is caught between two worlds–the one that handles blatant
acts of war like men, and the other which makes brown boys
eat their own tongues around these parts.

Today, he wipes up what he sees,
tucks his clothes into the supply closet,
out of sight. I catch the blood
in my throat that wants to burn the place down.

In two years from that day, my best friend will duck IEDs
to protect the owner's right to be a racist dick in a small town.
and maybe this is where brown folx are resigned to always be:

between a war and silence; between a wall and a country;
between your life, liberty and pursuit of happiness
at the cost of ours.

Stuck.

Once upon a time, I'd often sneak twenties and more
out from the register like immigrants who would breathe
freer in my pockets,
like the dead presidents would roll in their dead dirt
if they knew a Mexican had put his hands on them–stole them
in a stolen country.
I took until I was scared or until my anger was satisfied.

I was angry a lot then, bought Bob Marley records, learned the lyrics
to sing my soul on overtime shifts like field songs on the campesinos.
This is not a warrior's song. I was not Robin Hood.
This is me emulating the greed this country taught me.

I was young. I was angry.

I stole mad money from that Burger King.
And no matter how many times Bob Marley tells me not to be,
I am often afraid.

I worry about everything.

I worry for the next kid who gets hired

The Fourth Generation

> *they say the first generation sacrifices*
> *so that the second generation can achieve*
> *only for the third generation to squander*
> *and these third generation hands*
> *these hands have never picked cotton*
> -Amalia Ortiz

& the fourth generation is left to figure out the future

We couldn't build the hearth at the burning heart of the house
but we could set up Alexa to run the whole house

We didn't work 80 hour weeks
to send the children to school in white clean clothes
to keep the roof afloat in a sea of economic insecurity
to keep the beans boiling over the blue flame on the stove
but we work 80 hour weeks
to send ourselves to school
to keep the apartment afloat in a sea of economic insecurity
to keep the ramen noodles with sriracha at the ready
for hungry bellies of friends and girlfriends
lost family and strangers

We didn't pick cotton but we wore cotton
we wore the polished shoes
we saw our grandparents and loved them
saw our great-grandparents and missed them

saw our parents
saw the cul-de-sacs snap in half

the children boomerang back from the adult world
at a loss of self
at a loss for words
at a loss for purpose

We had hands ready to bleed and work
and we were given the internet
we had hands ready for revolution
and we were handed debt
we have hands we have these hands we have hands

We were given a holy world that was treated as if it were disposable
and then chided for not treating anything sacred

We were handed flaccid magic and expired spells
then blasted when the alchemy wouldn't take root
we carried broken child souls
to then be asked: what motivates us most? in college entrance essays

We saw a lowly sun and sad moon
return home every day at 5 pm

like all the life and love around us
was thrown down from the moon's height

yet still we hope

against fireflies that the world doesn't burn away before our hands can build something

If You Want to Know what it's like to be Mexican

III.

"Fresa" translated means "strawberry"
"Naco" means "ghetto"
Know which side of the divide you're on

There is always a division

There is always a divide

Loconuts

the name of this poem is:
for some reason when I say, "Donald Trump can suck my dick"
there's always another Mexicano telling me to chill
or
for some reason 23% of Latinos still support Donald Trump

or

if a Latino calls you a coconut that means
you're brown on the outside | white on the inside

or

a loconut is a pejorative   that I made up
that means you're brown on the outside
Donald Trump on the inside

or

the name of this poem is:
Loconuts please stop changing your names
from Esperanza to Hope
your last name says Si se Puede!
Your actions say Build that Wall!

Or

the name of this poem is:
Bougie Latinos play dead for survival
torn between the beaks of two eagles
they deny the violence
by pretending to be eagles themselves

toss down native tongues as welcome mats
saying: I'm not Mexican | I'm Spanish
knowing their abuelas
crossed the same fronteras
as our abuelas

or

the name of this poem is:
stop saying the barrio is a dangerous place to live
yes, my neighbor sells drugs and he's polite as shit

or

Loconuts, you're kinda low key part of the problem
or
you're kinda high key part of the problem
or
Latinos living under the veil of white privilege
you're kinda the fucking problem

or

the name of this poem is:
the god of irony taught us protecting murdered generations
meant teaching our children to be muted ghosts
catacombing our gods in the Earth of our throats

American history is a form of torture
that taught the people of the sun
to quit reaching for the sky

taught "being American" means "act respectable"
as a means to remain alive

we used to sacrifice still-beating hearts
to constellations
now when faced with a gun
we curb our fears
by pretending we are bullets too

Latinos are made of the morning
and the dying dusk
we are made of brighter things
that we were taught we weren't

"assimilation" is only a few letters away from "assed out"
we've turned our children into suburban flowers of assimilation

but no matter how many times we are plucked like weeds

gardens   still sprout   from the roots
being lost is no excuse for finding yourself
on the wrong side of the frontlines

or

The name of this poem is:
Latinos, I'm not saying that America is coming for you
I'm saying it already did
and when it wants to   again
loving Nascar
White Jesus
and naming your kid Brittney
won't save your ass anyway

Recetas
(Arroz Rojo)

Granted,
rice arrived like wheat arrived. The majority of what is dug up, grows, kills or dies comes from right here. The manteca is from here. The tomatoes are from here. The peppers. The maize. The sunflower. The cacao. All from here. The person you grow to be on these recipes comes from right here. What arrives should marry with, not murder out. Be itself. Be you–like red rice, your mother's, from her mother's, carrying so much from so far, from right here.

I'm a Shitty Gardener

At the risk of losing hood credibility
I pay the landscaper well

He doesn't do a good job but we both live here
And I want the neighborhood flourishing green and half-cut

Or at least to help the vato grab two beers
When the days done

My hands ruin the dirt
Make it rich for weeds

Sour for St Augustine
Green is not my fingertips destiny

I don't have much but I give as the good gods allow me
The gods gave me:

The driveway my father scraped his knee on
The smaller-than-average fireplace I broke an infant face on

Rooms where out-of-town family stayed
When in-town

I am always in-town now
My grandfather is on the other side of infinity

And I don't want him rolling up from so far away to cut the lawn

-I swear I'm on it-

Even if the whole house collapses
I will guard the front porch with my life
Handing out Capri Suns to the neighbor kids
During Sun Months bashing the green grass yellow and spotted

Note to self: buy a fucking sprinkler already

The Last Time I Saw You

/

A virtual family reunion. A wall of muted wails. Everyone takes their moment and machines run breath through your small body.

//

The second to last time I saw you:
I don't recall when exactly. Before Thanksgiving, I think, and I dropped by your yellow house.

I heard you sleep in the front room now--more manageable. Your bedroom: an unmoved, unchanged, mausoleum to the last 15 years. Why bother making the bed for lonely? Queen-sized, too large and heavy. I hugged you and said "goodbye, Little Lady." I snap a photo to send to my mother. You wore a Six Flags shirt with Wonder Woman on it.

///

The last time I do remember seeing you
I wandered off into the neighborhood awashed in psilocybin.

The way the world breathes content in its endlessness is a dare to let life go. The center of the universe emits out of everywhere. I walk under overcast skies, until the sun looks at me and I burn. Thirsty, I realized how close I am to Yellow House.

I pass San Fernando Cemetery #2. A grave digger sleeps on a yellow backhoe as still as a bed after a day of filling the earth with us. I arrive to your absence. I use the manguera like a boy baptizing a 36 year-old man. Preparing to leave and continue on, you arrive like mercy and I am a semi-crazed, wet dog. You invite me in. I sit. We dissolve in discussion like communion wafers on the tongue. You tell me exactly where everyone is at in their respective orbits. I down tap water from a mason jar. Before I leave, you ask if I need a ride. I decline. Opting for the air and the steps ahead.

A virus rages on unseen, outside. The world refuses to hold us delicately. The sky overcast again, and I put one foot in front of another. Goodbye, Little Lady.

If You Want to Know what it's like to be Mexican

IV.

    Lechuza
    perched on the corners of Catholic hearts–

    Oily white owl feathers
    do not engage

    madness of the mind
    do not engage

    a sickness
    we can't cuss our way out of

    a plague with no genesis point
    no exodus spell

    Hell is a place
    you live in when you are taught
    Heaven is a place
    you can be kept out of

    ignore her song
    do not engage

Bad Bird Mágico

It's bad magic when the thunderbird gets spotted in the Westside
a wingspan stretching telephone poles wide
bright curse feathers cruise & woosh over treelines
& reports come in from across the barrio

Jay saw it over by San Fernando Cemetery
Roy peeped it perched under Highway 90
Marie said she saw it feasting on the homeless
but we all know the thunderbird doesn't eat

it swoops & taunts
for a few months
then Roy gets a DUI
the crazy house pulls out all the flowers at night
Nikki dirties clean blood for the eighth time
every household wages a small war

the thunderbird reverse-phoenixes skyward
crackles & booms into a million lightning arcs
San Antonio floods
& we hope to never see it again

Gods like Us

the pope comes to San Antonio
undercover
witnessing our ways we
use day to day gods

for the day to day broken things:
dead batteries
suspended sentences
sueños aplastados
mala suerte regular as
roiling pots of refrito beans

asking our Christ for forgiveness
only on sabbath

and papa reveals himself
and asks why we do this?
¿why do we not turn to God every day?

and the people tell papa:
no. we turn to God every day
asking of him when the universe crumbles
aqui, papa, is for the regular
gods / gods who hurt
like us
dioses sin coronas
como nosotros

BO-DE-GAS

the corner stores where gasoline
is suspect
and the candy selection immigrated in
technicolor explosions more than all the candy stores
on the north side

and the men who look like roofing shingles
scorch-brown metal flashing tar burns and white
spackled like artists
come in breakfast rush and lunch breaks

stockpiling Mountain Dew in bathtub sized foam cups—
        the ones that die in abandoned lots for a generation

where children
who might never see Disneyland
point sweaty fingers at Mickey Mouse-faced ice cream
where spools of scratch-offs   find themselves
fortuitous as expired fruit

where women go to get out of the house
after the park with the babies and the compas
because goddamn it   it's hot   and they're thirsty

and I–in line–
examine the tattoo on the back of the man-in-front-of-me's head

petroglyphs   aged and distorted by black, bristle, buzz-cut stubble

what do we call that place?
where the cooked food looks eight degrees south of healthy
where customers carry on the faces of their fathers and mothers
this store where the pulse of the neighborhood beats until it closes
and the doors and windows shutter
with bars and
bulletproof locks?

is this where earth gathers and grows into people?

is this where god's hunger is never met but constantly fed?

Jury Duty Blues

my name   and all my information
are categorized and filed   somewhere   in this building
        the digital stenography of cameras   capture
every napkin   I put gum into   were I to lose
my mind   these agents could tell me who I am
down to the last   four digits of my social
security   everywhere   I notice
not a single   living   flower   exists in the
building   the air
another poem   the jury   exists because a
crime exists   a judge   exists because a law exists   we are
numbered and then changed   provided new numbers
was I 74 or 63?   was it better to be 74?
        what about me made me a 63 in the eyes of the court?
does my 63-ness say something   about my upbringing?
my mother?   this land is archived incorrectly   and yet
    this is the order of things
a boy stands accused   his mother
sits in the shadow of the accusation
like gum in a napkin   we are here now
neither party can return to what they were before
their atoms cannot untangle paper from elastomer   a fatal evening
from a mother's love   a date on a calendar   twelve
people selected   a law on a paper
a person unbodied   thank the chewing gum universe
I wasn't selected
some day in a calendar   a judge will open a sentence

and leave someone on the other side of it
some day in a calendar   a weapon   deleted
    all the days on the other side of it
I want to leave a flower behind   for any mother
    that needs it   after I go home
to the other side of a long day   and a woman in
a shadow   never leaves   her son

Rain, Humo, Rain

hearts crack and burst in summer like concrete or water mains
the sunshine
the day
the memories journaled on your notebook spirit
cannot hope to forget such a murderous sun

streets of black asphalt fire see

manguera children
raining water like falling candy

a sun-dried couple
ashing a shared cigarette outside the door frame of a cantina
shady and full of cold beer and hot cheetos

grandmothers
sitting in front of box fans with a tray of hot cafecito and pan dulce

a dj at midnight
waiting for cues from crowds to drown them
in sex and dance and love music

–all surviving another cruel summer in the haze and fire
in each day's searing battery

and I am a long melody laid on top of it–
a boy in search of a big red on his bicycle
or a pond to jump

Kool Kool Guy

or
Wild shit happens all the time in the hood and sometimes it's real and sometimes it's not

Rainy November sits on the city's skin like the cold ocean.
I am shambling on its shoulders towards the corner store.

Across the way,
I spot Rodney–
The loco vato from my barrio
Who swears on crystals, astrology, ptsd and Bud Light,
And he is soaked in the same wet as I am.

Rodney aflame with something on his mind,
Runs up on me–jaywalking, crossing 4 lanes and dodging 6 cars going 30;
He says: Roost, you're not gonna believe it
I say: What foo?
He says: I saw Kool Kool Guy.
I say: who?
He says:

> Kool Kool Guy. I was out by Woodlawn Lake and three dudes were trying to jump me when SPLASH! The ducks and geese trip out, the ravens and grackles flew off, the tadpoles and turtles start acting crazy, and out the pinche lago, este vato, Kool

Kool Guy wey! He had on some fresh Adidas chanclas con alas and everything.
Chewm Chewm Chewm!
He was flying and jumping and flying and jumping, color bronce and scared away the three vatos trying to beat my ass. He flew down all like and was all like 'wus up, foo?'
And I said, 'I ain't got no beef, homie. But yo, those flying chanclas you got on are super fly.' Homie looked like a young Edward James Olmos mixed with Carlos Santana
He had on all this gold jewelry like Mexican Mr. T and stuff like dude was not scared of getting robbed by nobody,
And I was like, 'so you from around here or what foo?'
And he was like 'nah'
He was like 'I'm from the O-cean' and I said 'oh shit, Corpus?'
He was like, 'nah, I run all of that water'
He said, 'my enemies call me Namor but my people call me Kool Kool Guy'
And I'm wondering who's messing with someone named Kool Kool Guy with wings on his feet but whatever, everybody's got haters I guess. And then, a turtle came up to the homie and started

whispering to him. I couldn't understand the turtle, but I could tell it was something serious. I ask Kool Kool Guy wus up, did he need backup or what?
And he was like 'how long can you hold your breath?'

    I told him regular amount but I'm down to try
    And he said, nah, some other time,
      then dove off and Kool Kool Guy was gone!

And I said: Rodney, what have you been smoking?
And he swore on his unemployment check that it happened,
And we both stood in the rain,
But only one of us saw a miracle through all the water.

My Bank Emails Me and Asks if I'm Ready to Plan for My Retirement

Do you watch trash TV
as a mode of escapism for economic insecurity?
Me too.
Watching Million Dollar Listings Los Angeles,
I see Rolls Royces driving on streaks of sunlight and ocean spray worth more
than the ruined houses my neighborhood houses;
I see haircuts that could feed a family of five for five months;
enough botox to fix the cracks and potholes along my stray-dog-lined streets.
I see an Eden full of food and dessert,
endless sauvignon blanc–the opposite of the food desert I live in.

How long did I live on peanut butter and a single slice of bread,
tacos of potatoes and eggs?
And I don't care how much you fancify it, I refuse to eat spam to this day.

My bank emails me and asks if I am ready to plan for my retirement–
I'm 39 and just kinda started earning a living.

There are a few born to financial freedom and alive.
For the majority, we are born mid-stride–
outrunning the clock, the hounds, the hours and overtime,
clocking graveyard shifts for a ghost of an extra paycheck.

Oh what it must feel like:

to know how a fingertip / glides in worlds of marble

to never have eaten economic insecurity,
to not temper flame and forge your own iron in a dark age.

At what point in earning all this living do we get to live, y'all?
Why is cutthroat capitalism always feast or famine?
I say: Let's take the tools they gave
and feast away our famine on the rich.

But I'm not actually saying eat the rich, I'm saying: rob them.
Because this is for those who stretch a few cents into a sacred lunch,
for the hands hoping the paycheck clears at midnight,
for the haters of insufficient funds fees
for those with ten toes on the broke-and-barely-hanging-on
side of the rainbow.

We are not rich but we're here–

sometimes all we can afford is a hallelujah
sometimes the only way out of a depression
is to stop killing yourself to live
sometimes alive and unbothered
is all the wealth we keep.

Barrio Yard Sale

> *A group piece co-written with Chibbi Orduña &*
> *Andrea "Vocab" Sanderson*

The price is right
It's just a little too...
"Ethnic"

Home buyers: Looking for a new place to live?
The ghetto!
The barrio!
The hood!
For Sale! Everyone must go!

Where we live is moving up in the world
Even if we are not.
Property value going up!
Skyline going up!
Tax brackets going up!
Rent going up!

House Hunters & HGTV has people thinking the American dream
isn't causing a nightmare
Neighborhoods that used to be police targets are now target markets
Martin Luther King Blvd looking like
Alamo Whites, I mean Alamo Heights

"Moving on up to the east side"

For those of you privileged enough to afford it
Flip or Flop a Fixer Upper,
sell it off while it's still a commodity,
while these neighborhoods are still in vogue,
and we can all be: Property Brothers!

We might as well cash grab on our way out the door
before the gringos remember that
tequila is not their friend.

Because everyone feels real cultured when they go to
¡¡¡Chipotle!!!
…
¡¡¡¿¿¿Chipotle???!!!

Cultural appropriation is the new colonization.
We gotta Love It or List It
while these stereotypes are still smokin' hot!

Here,
take these creased and khaki-clad vatos,
bleach 'em white
and they'll fit in perfectly with that refined urban gait.

Watch gated communities
take the place of the projects.

House flipping is sending the local economy into somersaults.
Better get in while the gettin' is good to be got.
Macklemore dropped one hit and now,
we can't get shit from the thrift shop.

Nevermind the families on a fixed income,
get your fixer upper in the hood
you didn't want us as neighbors in the 90s,
but now you are cashing in your 401k for my Section 8,

Didn't realize your White Flight was a round trip,

Didn't realize your idea of retail value was color coded,

Didn't realize when you arrived with Bibles
saying "Love thy Neighbor"
you were getting the neighbors the fuck outta here.

Gentrification is another form of deportation,
Dressing up your arrival like a Thanksgiving turkey
When it tastes more like Manifest Destiny.
We've been through this already!

The colonizers arrived to build a better New World,
but did anyone stop to ask
what was wrong
with the old one?

Our people built families on this land
long before you decided to build shopping centers!
Don't tell me to go back to where I came from
when the border crossed me, motherfucker!

Brokers are breaking up our history
weaponizing real estate and erasing   us   out
one block at a time

The ghetto,
the barrio,
the neighborhood,
SOLD!

Pack up your languages and loved ones
and don't let the closing costs hit you
on the way
out

The Legend of Mark

Men, gentle ladies, & bomb ass non-binary folk
permit me to tell you about an urban legend
the size of South Texas.
If we're lucky, perhaps this amazing apparition
will appear tonight.
Because like Sasquatch belongs to the forested Northwest
and Nessie belongs to Loch Ness,
this cryptozoological mystery figure is often found
on the St Mary's Strip.

Like all miracles, he appears when you least expect—
when you're six Lone Stars, five chamoy shots,
four ocean waters, three hits from the magic vape pen,
two random make out sessions,
and one "okay, okay, okay bitch, a last shot of tequila"
in.

It's then
through the American Spirit smoke and bloodshot eyes,
when your stomach is a wild chupacabra,
the angel of the strip arrives—
the Pizza Classics Pizza Guy.

He is the pepperoni and cheese apostle of Christ.
The physical embodiment of all six infinity stones.
He is the courier qualified to carry canapés worthy of champions,
parading the pizzas our 2 am, turnt and needing to sober up

asses are addicted to. And yes, I'm an addict just like you.

I too have found empty Pizza Classics boxes in the backseat
not knowing how they got there after a long night
of Andrew poured libations.
I too have vaguely seen the silhouette
of a backwards hat and pizza bag.
I too have questioned, if he was real or the imagined fever
dream of too much whiskey.
But my fellow people, allow me to say,
The Pizza Classics Pizza Guy is REAL!

For six bucks, he will heal you
when your eyes are bigger than the bar.
For six bucks, he will slide you a greasy slice
to suck up all the Angry Orchard Apple Cider you imbibed.
For six bucks, he will avail you from the evil
of all the shots you took
While Lil Jon sang Shots, Shots, Shots, Shots!

He saves your Wednesday from being a horrible hangover
Thursday because he isn't walking miles and miles of mercy
on the North Side or the Eastside or the Westside
he walks all those miles carrying all those pizzas
because he's on our side
and your side.

And if you were to ask me if the pizza is any good,
I'd say "good is relative
asshole."
But I will say, that when you're upside down
on all sorts of liquor, it's six bucks,
it's right on time, and life deserves affordable magic.

So keep your eyes peeled for this mer-pizza-maid
and trust it is no illusion.
After a deluge into high proof alcohol,
he is the alpha and omega of all things circular and boxed.
He is the alien abduction that ends in pizza crust.
The Phantom of the Strip. Mother Teresa to us misfits.
Drink responsibly, tip graciously, and get home safely.

Mexican Dinosaur

After a friend wonders if Quetzalcóatl was the Aztecan concept for dinosaurs

Yes and
Anubis is the Egyptian Wolfman
Christ is the Gringo-Neo in the Matrix

Only USA myths are real

The Romans murdered Christ and from his blood
America

Only gods of fair skin–
Not scales and feathers–
Matter.

Only a triumvirate god and spirit and son can birth a universe
A Mexican Dinosaur is merely a cute story
Or a mistake

If You Want to Know what it's like to be Mexican

V.

Of course   there is no gravity
there is no flag to fall under
there is no land that is ours

There never was
And that's the magic

Our names are our names
Branded on us though they may be

We carry ourselves as ourselves

You put a Westsider on the moon
They'll still walk a certain way

Ten Things About South Texas of which I am Certain

1.
South Texas ends at Thousand Oaks and 281,
and your worldview lacks magic
if you don't love us,

& Six Gawd sells the best weed.

2.
For a city without seasons, we're rife with color—
green, brown, black and silver, and the messed-up neon colors
the Spurs used to be
—streaking across this city every night.

San Antonio is a hungry universe full of floodlight people.

3.
And the weathermen should be shot;
they can't predict nada,
can't predict if the rain will fall or the sun will rise.

4.
I didn't have my first:
date / kiss / dance / drink / Love / here

surprisingly, all of it gets better here.
Trust me.

& Six Gawd sells the best weed.

V.
Laredo is where you drink
when you are certain you want to sweat
and drown. Where you forget
that you have somewhere to go back to.
Where you are allowed to lay your burden down,
bleed everything out over a dance record,
and they will love you all the same.

The Rio Grande Valley is the Rio Grande Valley.
And truthfully, I don't know a lot about the RGV
except that their number one export is cool people to San Antonio.

6.
We are the throughway for the migration of monarchs—
maybe we are royal,
maybe we are only passing through before we die,
so we make our fingerprints into good memories,
place our wings on everything

7.
The politicians brand new area codes into us;
file old streets under new names.
Forgetting is a prayer our hands do not know;
We never get all the dirt and blood

and memories, from under our nails, out.

8.
Around Lackland, there are seasons, one will see
a flood of newly minted airmen and women
at Applebees
with their families–

scared children who look like new brass.
Welcome to this river and its song.

9.
and we don't understand 30 degree weather | and I know there will be times when a kiss will feel like old magic | and we are so often past places we once stood in | call me: apt. 285, Bent Tree, Fredericksburg rd. 78240 | with second hand furniture | a mountain of cigarettes in the ashtray and a Jimi Hendrix poster stapled on the wall | call me, my dead grandmother's house 78237

and I know only one person who owns a house that didn't previously belong to family | owning a new house is for rich men | (and teachers who need to put their frustrated energy into something productive and not beating your bad ass kids) | and who has time to be a rich man when there is all this Lone Star?

we are not drunk; we are festive, all the time.

X.

And people will die here and love here and continue on here.

And the politicians will predict an onslaught of new residents

Forecasting   a future where the city looks like Houston
/ Austin / Atlantis / El Dorado.

My tio says:
Chale', they don't know nothing
like the weatherman.

They don't know that we've been gold.
Being who we are means we don't act like anyone else's song.

& Six Gawd sells the best weed.

Sunflower Road

off highway 151 and callaghan
there is a street that ends in sunflowers

i imagine a city developer
with a heart of seeds
dreamt to conquer a dead end
& so it was
& so can we

everyday
so can we

I GOT KICKED OUT OF COLLEGE THREE TIMES AND STILL ARRIVED ON THIS SIDE OF GLASS

the landscaper smells of lawn mower gas
and cut grass matted on sweat denim
takes a drag off of the cigarette he'd asked me for
says something along the lines of
never seen you around here before now

he keeps the conversation light
cherry flame carving through the white paper
and tobacco   his lungs are rust
i brown mine with him

he works the grounds of the ivory campus
says it's good to see a Chicano up there
like we got away with a smooth heist
i say

couldn't let the wrong things keep me
on the bad side of forever

órale
he says

makes me proud
and i don't even know you

my father told me of people

i'd likely never meet or
never know   who made it possible
for my feet to stand
at the vanguard of sky and broken glass
here

and during our conversation   we discover
we come from the same side
of the under glass   streets away
if i had hit a home run from my front porch
i could break his window

and fresh cut grass and gasoline
are all I remember of my father some days
he   a battery maker
put a baseball in my shoes hit a home run

i'm feeling the boombox of life throwing chingasos as
both of our cigarettes die slow as hourglasses of fire
the landscaper and i know more myths
than people who made it out
his hands are not unlike my grandfathers
like deer splayed on the side of the road

today my legs carry fresh smoke
and he and i come from a side of town that lights up
every new year and fourth of july

better than the city's fireworks downtown

on nights when our surnames are not crackling over radios
for all-points bulletins
nor teachers punishing the language
our fathers worked 60-hour-work-weeks for
out of us
on those nights
there is red   white   and blue
streaming from our skies
the firmament   open

Chingasos from Above

Don't take my demeanor, quieter because of my age—
now getting up in numbers,
these poorly constructed knees,
and bad vision—for pacifist.

I still carry Texas indigo snake fists
beating back the ruined rattlesnake gods.

There are reasons worth leaving
earth early that I'm still in search of.

Were I able to grab hold a cloud and watch
humankind deconstruct itself for decades,
I'd still rain chingasos from sky,
rim the world with salt in a tequila shot of its own pain.

I would break apart a cruel planet for a kinder one
so one kid could feel like they never had to raise a fist,
or flip coke to attack the lack at the heart of their misery,
so one kid can sit in their own skin as comfortably
as I sit in my own,
so one kid can see the tomorrow of their dreams.

These one-kids are many
and so I fight, volcan,
and pray the hot blood I leave behind—
my own or some devil's—
makes better ground for others to stand on.

A Confederacy of Ghosts Still Here

||SATX||

Abuelita warns of the ghosts still here
Who camp underneath our beds

Ripped to shreds by daylight
Cause the floorboards to creak
Something awful

||CENTRAL TEXAS||

Here
Distance is measured in time

I don't know how far
The town   you don't stop

For gas or ice or hospitality
Or otherwise   is

But it's less than thirty-minutes
That way   in every direction

Move
Or stay put

And pray the wind

                                                Won't raise the floors

||SATX||

Here
Young vato never stepped foot
A second outside the city

Swears he knows what's up
Talks that way

Wants outta here

Wants somewhere else

Wants the world

I hope he never finds
Forty-minutes north

Stays full of the city
That quarters him

I hope he is a ghost
To ghosts

When he stops for gas
When his hair is burnt sage

And his skin is seen
As if for the first time

By the country
Ahead of him

If You Want to Know what it's like to be Mexican

VI.

        a
        silent luxury

        like

                  stars
        reflected
        in
            cool   miracle
            waters
            of
                dark
                cenotes–

                subterranean
                &
                heavenly

                both

I Grew Tired of the Old Gods, so I Made New Ones

In the beginning was the big nothing,
And the big nothing knew all, saw all, heard all, but did nothing.
And the big nothing grew bored, so the big nothing
Got high one day and spat out the prime gods: Chuy and Reina
(and they weren't related or pulled from the others' rib
Or any other weird shit like that).

And Chuy was Reina's viejo
And Reina was Chuy's ruca
And they cruised the blank nothing
In his cosmic ranfla.

And one day, the ship got a blowout
And rode on the rim too long–
The sparks got stuck and became stars.
And one day, the ship backfired,
And the smoke and bang
Made galaxies and planets.

And Reina, being the ever cool deity she is,
Painted those stars into sick constellations
And painted creatures and landscapes on those lonely planets.
And Chuy fell even more in love,
And they had three children–
Flaca, Gordo, and Humo.

Flaca was a girl
Gordo was a boy
Humo was neither.

And Flaca was made of clumsy earthquakes
And Gordo was made of the rolling ocean
And Humo was made of cleansing smoke and rain

And on this planet
All the animals of night
(before night was night)
Came from everywhere
Held a meeting
The jackal and the owl
The snake and the raccoon
The jaguar and the possum
The tarantula and the bat
The scorpion and others
And they all agreed that they couldn't see shit
So they voted for the wolf to talk to Chuy
And the wolf howled and told Chuy
The darkness was too much
So Chuy agreed and punched a hole in the night
And the moon shone through
And the animals thanked him
And once in a while, the wolf howls to remind Chuy
On the nights he's too drunk

And forgets to let the moon out.

And Chuy is the type of vato
Who only pays attention to what he cares about
So when the pine trees and grass
Cacti and bush begged
For their own holy light
Chuy was always busy doing something
Which was probably nothing
So Reina
Heard their songs and smiled
She kissed Chuy and the children while they slept
And she left to become the Sun

Now what would later become the devil
Began as Chuy's sad shadow
How it grew and draped over his son
Gordo never knew how to get out of it
So Gordo built worlds made of feelings in the shadows
And in those worlds became envy
And in envy came a twisted voice
And the twisted voice was el pinche cienpiés
And each of its thousands of legs carried evil
And each bite was a cruel poison
And el cienpiés crawled out of the shadows
And into the rest of the universe.

Somos Cosmicanos

we are the makers of old magic
the have been & the always will be

la gente de las semillas
lluvia
y sol

hand in hand we
carry each other beyond cosmos

& I would love to say one word—
una palabra—

could capture all our lightning essence
Latina, Latino, Latine, Hispanic, Latinx

sabes que—you can't.
one word ain't enough—

like Love like Love like Love
one word ain't enough

Wasim Akram and Allen Iverson on the Blacktop

The men,
originally from
Pakistan,
brought cricket
to this side
of town.
And before dusk—
when the fire crown
South Texas wears
drops low enough
to ease the scorch,
everyday,
multitudes play
in polo shirts
and faux leather
belts, soft
walmart loafers,
in khaki shorts
too short
for Allen Iverson.
And yes,
even here
in Countdown City,
we salute the 5'11" god.
And yes,
Mexican kids
wore straight backs

in support of the god.

And yes,
I am
Mexican kids.

At almost
6 feet tall,
I am one
of the fortunate
souls able to jump
to touch rim–

most homies
here
only touch net.
And we ball
between 4
and dusk.
We bang hard
in this small
melting
of America,
rising
and rising
and rising
in the waves of heat,

putting up jumpers
—wet—
flooding
burnt August.
And all the sweat
erases
the lack
at home
like Mount Mutombo
waving his finger
as if to say:
Not today,
in his blacktop gravel voice.
(He
also
an immigrant.)
Moving back
here
to go to school,
my secret was—
I was never leaving
again.
Two games
share the blacktop;
the occasional
stray
cricket ball

or missed pass
pauses
play
of each others'
sport,
but they ball and we ball.

Occasionally,
their onlookers
cheer our game
and,
occasionally,
we watch them—
ignorant
to when cricket warrants applause.
And at these hours,
in this gravel
heat,
you never can tell
who sweats
more
or who earned a spot
to play.

Acknowledgements

I'd like to give immense gratitude to Chibbi Orduña and Ayokunle Falomo for their editing mastery on this project and to Write About Now Poetry for providing a home for these works. I'd like to thank my family (three scorpions, a centaur, and a fish), and my family who walk on the other side of the universe.

The epigraph in "Fourth Generation" comes from the poem "these hands which have never picked cotton" by Amalia Ortiz.

An original draft of "Barrio Yard Sale" was written by me. The poem was eventually turned into a group poem with contributions by Eddie Vega, Chibbi Orduña, Ariel Cottingham, and Andrea "Vocab" Sanderson.

Voices de la Luna: "Recetas (Salsa Verde)" and "Black Fur"

Huizache: "Kool Kool Guy" and "Wasim Akrim and Allen Iverson on the Blacktop"

The Acentos Review: "The last time I saw you"

ABOUT THE AUTHOR

C.L. "Rooster" Martinez is an educator, writer and spoken word poet from San Antonio, Texas. He is the author of two poetry books: A Saint for Lost Things (Alabrava Press, 2020) and As it is in Heaven (Kissing Dynamite Poetry Press, 2020), as well as an upcoming kid's book *PURO GLXY DFNDR* through Juventude Press. His work has appeared in such publications as Huizache, Voices de la Luna, Write About Now Poetry, Button Poetry, The Huffington Post Latino Voices, The Acentos Review, and others. He is co-editor on Contra: Texas Poets Speak Out, a poetry anthology, and was a writer on the 2016 play, American Pride, which won two ATAC Globe awards for Writing of a Drama and Overall Production of a Drama. Rooster earned a MA/MFA in Creative Writing, Literature and Social Justice from Our Lady of the Lake University and teaches English at Palo Alto College.

Suggested Playlist

This playlist is full of rock & roll, punk, and metal tracks that felt in the same spiritual vein as Mexican Dinosaur.
- Rooster

On Spotify

On YouTube

Other Titles by C.L. "Rooster" Martinez

PURO GLXY DFNDR, Juventud Press, forthcoming
Contra: Texas Poets Speak Out, Flowersong Press, 2020
A Saint for Lost Things, Alabrava Press, 2020
As it is in Heaven, Kissing Dynamite Poetry Press, 2020

Other Titles by Write About Now

We All Make it Out in the End by Lacey Roop
Golden Brown Skin by S.C. Says
OTRO/PATRIA by M.R. "Chibbi" Orduña
Going Down Singing by Kevin Burke
They Rewrote Themselves Legendary by Ronnie K. Stephnes
Universe in the Key of Matryoshka by Ronnie K. Stephens
Rebel Hearts & Restless Ghosts by William James
And then Came the Flood by Lacey Roop

www.ingramcontent.com/pod-product-compliance
Lightning Source LLC
Chambersburg PA
CBHW010447010526
44118CB00021B/2535